WHSmith

National Test Practice Papers

English Level 6

Christine Moorcroft and Ray Barker

Age 10–11
Year 6
Key Stage 2

The Publishers would like to thank the following for permission to reproduce copyright material:

'Budgerigars and begonias', website extract from *http://www.medicine.ox.ac.uk/bandolier/band34/b34-5.html*
Jenny Joseph: 'Warning' from *Selected Poems* (Bloodaxe Books, 1992), copyright © Jenny Joseph, reproduced by permission of Johnson & Alcock
Standards and Testing Agency: What does a Level 6 look like in writing? – simplified descriptions (Department for Education). Permission for re-use of all © Crown copyright information is granted under the terms of the Open Government Licence (OGL)
Dylan Thomas: from *Portrait of the Artist as a Young Dog* (J. M. Dent, 1940), copyright © The Trustees for the copyrights of the late Dylan Thomas 1940, reproduced by permission of David Higham Associates

Every effort has been made to trace all copyright holders, but if any have been inadvertently overlooked the Publishers will be pleased to make the necessary arrangements at the first opportunity.

Although every effort has been made to ensure that website addresses are correct at time of going to press, Hodder Education cannot be held responsible for the content of any website mentioned in this book. It is sometimes possible to find a relocated web page by typing in the address of the home page for a website in the URL window of your browser.

Hachette UK's policy is to use papers that are natural, renewable and recyclable products and made from wood grown in sustainable forests. The logging and manufacturing processes are expected to conform to the environmental regulations of the country of origin.

Orders: please contact Bookpoint Ltd, 130 Milton Park, Abingdon, Oxon OX14 4SB. Telephone: (44) 01235 827720. Fax: (44) 01235 400454. Lines are open 9.00a.m.–5.00p.m., Monday to Saturday, with a 24-hour message answering service. Visit our website at www.hoddereducation.co.uk.

© Christine Moorcroft and Ray Barker 2013
First published in 2013 exclusively for WHSmith by
Hodder Education
An Hachette UK Company
338 Euston Road
London NW1 3BH

Impression number   10 9 8 7 6 5 4 3 2
Year   2018 2017 2016 2015 2014 2013

All rights reserved. Apart from any use permitted under UK copyright law, no part of this publication may be reproduced or transmitted in any form or by any means, electronic or mechanical, including photocopying and recording, or held within any information storage and retrieval system, without permission in writing from the publisher or under licence from the Copyright Licensing Agency Limited. Further details of such licences (for reprographic reproduction) may be obtained from the Copyright Licensing Agency Limited, Saffron House, 6–10 Kirby Street, London EC1N 8TS.

Cover illustration by Oxford Designers and Illustrators Ltd
Typeset by DC Graphic Design Ltd, Swanley Village, Kent
Printed in Great Britain by Hobbs the Printers Ltd, Totton, Hampshire SO40 3WX

A catalogue record for this title is available from the British Library.

ISBN: 978 1444 189 223

NOTE: The tests, questions and advice in this book are not reproductions of the official test materials sent to schools. The official testing process is supported by guidance and training for teachers in setting and marking tests and interpreting the results. The results achieved in the tests in this book may not be the same as are achieved in the official tests.

Contents

Useful Information

National Tests in English at Age 11	v
How to use this book	vi
Working through the tests	viii

The Tests

Introduction to the Reading Test	x
Reading Test	1
Introduction to the Writing Test	13
Writing Test	14
Grammar, Punctuation and Spelling Test	16

Answers, Marking and Conversion Tables

Answers to the Reading Test	24
Assessing the Writing Test	30
Answers to the Grammar, Punctuation and Spelling Test	34

National Curriculum Levels – Level 6   36

Introduction

National Tests in English at Age 11

Testing children's progress at the end of Key Stage 2 (age 11)

All children enrolled at maintained schools or at Academies (including Free Schools), who will have completed the Key Stage 2 programme of study in the 2012/13 school year, must be registered for the tests. All children working at Level 3 or above must take the tests, unless they have taken the tests in the past.

Most of the children taking the tests will be in Year 6 and will reach the age of 11 by the end of the school year. This includes children with special educational needs (SEN) who will start some aspects of the Key Stage 3 programme of study without having completed all of the Key Stage 2 programme of study.

In addition, schools can administer Level 6 tests in English reading, writing and mathematics. These tests are optional and are aimed at high-attaining children.

Schools have been asked to keep the weeks commencing 13 and 20 May 2013 free for administering the Key Stage 2 tests.

Children are tested for four main purposes:

- to enable their teachers to make plans for their learning
- to find any problems or areas with which the children need extra help
- to show the children what they have learned and help them to think about their own learning
- to compare their achievement with what is expected.

The results of the tests inform:

- children about their own progress
- parents about their children's progress
- teachers about the progress of each child and of the class as a whole
- headteachers and school governors about the performance of the school
- the local education authority and the Office for Standards in Education about the performance of different schools.

The ways in which children are tested:

- National Tests at age 11
- formal teacher assessment at age 7, 11 and 14
- day to day, week to week, month to month and term to term notes and records kept by the teacher (including marks for written work and notes about other activities) so that he or she can build up a picture of each child's progress.

Levels

- The marks given to each child in the National Tests in English are used to find out his or her National Curriculum level. The levels go from 1 up to 8 for children's achievement between the ages of 5 and 16. Most children progress through one level in two years.
- The teacher's formal assessment is also recorded as a "level".
- The main Key Stage 1 tests cover up to Level 3 (there are also special arrangements for Level 4 tests for the most able children). The nationally expected level for Year 6 children is Level 4. **For the small number of children who attain Level 5 easily, there is a special Level 6 test as provided in this book**.
- Please note that the tests, questions and advice in this book are not reproductions of the official tests. The official testing process is supported by guidance and training for teachers in setting, marking and moderating tests and your child's work, as well as interpreting the results. This means that the results achieved in this book may not be the same as those achieved in the official tests.

Introduction

How to use this book

The purposes of this book

- To prepare children working at a higher level for National Tests in English by giving them practice, so that they will be familiar with the form of the tests they will take.

- Level 6 papers will be aimed at very able 11-year-olds, whose work in class is at the standard expected of a 14-year-old.

- To help parents to judge their children's progress in English. Results of the tests will feature in league tables of primary schools' performance. Secondary schools will also be informed of which children pass the test, to ensure they end up in the top sets.

The practice tests

This book includes practice tests and tasks on Reading, Writing and Grammar, Punctuation and Spelling.

Answers and a marking schedule are provided in the centre of the book. General instructions for all the tests are given.

Specific instructions for each test are given in the introduction to that test.

The Reading Test at Level 6

Most children take the Level 3–5 test, but those working at a higher level are catered for in this book.

For the English reading test, 10 minutes of reading time is provided with 50 minutes to answer the questions.

Types of question set in the Reading Test

The Reading Test comprises a variety of texts – perhaps non-fiction, fiction and poetry – to test reading strategies across a range of genres. There will normally be a link or a common theme between the passages. The questions require three different kinds of answer:

- Short words or phrases only. Usually one mark is allocated for each correct response.

- Longer answers – one or two sentences. Usually two marks are allocated for these answers, as they require more understanding of the text.

- Detailed explanations of opinion. These are longer and involve a more personal approach. Up to five marks are allocated.

Incorrect answers are given a zero score and no half marks are awarded.

Although some of the questions will have a "right answer", all children will express their responses in a different way. When marking the questions, look for the content of what has been written and not just the quality of the writing, grammar, etc.

Introduction

The Writing Test at Level 6

There are three aspects to consider in your child's achievement in writing:

1. Organisation and purpose (the content of the story or, in information writing, the form and content of the text).
2. Grammar (the correct use of punctuation, capital letters, tenses and pronouns).
3. Style (use of connective words, sentence structure and vocabulary).

Your child might do better in one of these aspects than in the others. Looking at his or her writing in this way helps to pinpoint strengths and weaknesses.

The Level 6 internally marked English Writing Test consists of two tasks in a single paper:

- a Shorter Writing Task
- a Longer Writing Task.

Children should take both the Shorter Writing and Longer Writing Tasks in a single sitting.

Marks from both tasks will be needed in order to assess whether the child is working at Level 6 in English writing.

Children should be given an hour for this test. It is recommended that they are given 20 minutes for the Shorter Writing Task and 40 minutes for the Longer Writing Task (including up to five minutes of planning time).

A planning sheet is not provided for the Shorter Writing Task, but children may use blank paper if they wish to plan. A planning sheet is provided for the Longer Writing Task.

Speaking and listening are not currently tested, but levels are reported as part of teacher assessment judgements.

The Grammar, Punctuation and Spelling Test

The new test will put an additional focus on essential skills. Children should have mastered these skills by the time they leave primary school, so that they can enter secondary school with the basic skills in place.

The Grammar, Punctuation and Spelling Test will only include questions that assess elements of the current English curriculum. It will cover:

- sentence grammar (through identification and grammatical accuracy)
- punctuation (through identification and grammatical accuracy)
- vocabulary (through grammatical accuracy)
- spelling.

Introduction

Working through the tests

Tests and exams can be very stressful, mainly because people do not like to feel judged by others – especially if they feel that the results may not be as good as others expect.

The tests in this book are modelled as closely as possible on the real thing so that pupils will not be surprised by the test format. However, parents can help them to cope with the pressure of the tests by using the material in this book as a resource for teaching and learning. Share the experiences, questions and discussions that arise from the tests. You could even try sitting one yourself!

Some important points

- A relaxed approach is best. If you feel anxious, your child will sense this and might not concentrate or perform as well as he or she could.

- Work in a quiet place where you and your child will not be distracted.

- Before beginning the tests you might find it useful to make a copy of pages 1 and 13 for your reference while your child writes in this book.

- Your child will need a pencil and, if possible, an eraser; if you do not have an eraser, ask your child to cross out any mistakes made. Please reinforce the idea that your child will not lose marks if he or she crosses out work. Many children fear that tidiness is the major criterion for success in these tests. Although legibility and clarity are assessed, planning and drafting are encouraged.

- Provide some extra paper – although note that some answers need to be completed in the book.

- Do not provide resources that will help in the test, such as a dictionary.

- Do not ask your child to do all the tests one after the other without a break between each one.

- Encourage your child and give praise for what he or she can do.

- Do not dwell on what he or she cannot do but, at another time, you could provide practice in the areas where it is needed. Be guided by your child's teacher as to what are the best ways in which you can help.

- Timing is important. Encourage children to move on to another question if time appears to be running out. It is bad practice to concentrate on one question just because the candidate is in possession of the "answer" or because the child is enjoying the experience!

- Get the child into the habit of checking all work before the test is finished.

What do the results mean?

The National Curriculum conversion charts on page 36 show how the marks for these tests are converted to National Curriculum levels. Performance in any test in the book should be regarded only as a guide. It does not guarantee the same result from the actual test.

- Practice helps your child to feel comfortable with the process of taking tests (while also helping to improve his or her knowledge, understanding and skills in English).

- No one is motivated by being told that he or she has "failed". Instead use the experience gained from this book to improve performance.

- It is best to give your child a break between each test.

- Your child should write on the test copy on pages 6 to 12 and 14 to 23.

Introduction

- At the end of the test enter his or her mark for each question in the circle provided (the number indicates the possible mark).
- The answers are on pages 24 to 35.
- National Curriculum Levels are given on page 36.

The Reading Test (pages 1 to 12)

1. Ask your child to turn to the Reading Test (page 1).
2. Encourage him or her to read the text carefully.
3. Point out the two different types of question: those that give a choice of answers, one of which is ticked, and those that ask for a written answer. Written answers need not be complete sentences. Some of the written answers are awarded three or more marks if detail or examples are required.
4. Do not help your child to read the rest of the text. Encourage your child to take care, but point out that he or she may rub out or alter any mistakes made.
5. Tell the child:
   - to find the answers in the text, rather than giving answers which he or she already knows
   - to tick only one box to answer each question
   - to have a try at answering every question
   - to leave any questions he or she cannot answer, and go back to them at the end
   - to re-read the text to find the answers to questions.
6. Allow your child to read the text independently and to answer the questions without any help.

Introduction to the Reading Test

On the following pages there are different types of question for you to answer in different ways. The space for your answer shows you what type of writing and how much is needed.

1. **Short answers**

    Some questions are followed by one line. This shows that you need only write a word or a phrase in your answer. Sometimes you may have to tick or draw a line.

2. **Several line answers**

    Some questions are followed by two or three lines. This gives you space to write more words or a sentence or two.

3. **Longer answers**

    Some questions are followed by more than three lines. This shows that a longer, more detailed answer is needed to explain your opinion. You should try to write in full sentences.

Marks

The number under each circle in the margin tells you the maximum number of marks for each question.

Please wait until you are told to start work on this test. You should work through the question until you are asked to stop, referring to the passages in your test when you need to.

Good luck!

Reading Test

- The paper is **1** hour long.

- You have **10** minutes to read the texts before answering the questions. During this time you should not start to write.

- You then have **50** minutes to write your answers.

- Answer all the questions.

- There are **15** questions totalling **50** marks on this paper.

- Check your work carefully.

Don't be afraid to underline or circle or highlight the key points in the texts as you are reading them. You can write in the margin of the booklets, too.

The theme linking these three passages is "old people".

Passage 1

The passage comes from Dylan Thomas's autobiography and tells of a visit to his grandfather's.

In the middle of the night I woke from a dream full of whips, lariats as long as serpents, and runaway coaches on mountain passes, and wide, windy gallops over cactus fields, and I heard the old man in the next room crying, "Gee-up!" and "Whoa!" and trotting his tongue on the roof of his mouth.

It was the first time I had stayed in grandpa's house. The floorboards had creaked like mice as I climbed into bed, and the mice between the walls had creaked like wood as though another visitor was walking on them. It was a mild summer night, but curtains had flapped and branches beaten against the window. I had pulled the sheets over my head, and soon was roaring and riding in a book.

"Whoa there, my beauties!" cried grandpa. His voice sounded very young and loud, and his tongue had powerful hooves, and he made his bedroom into a great meadow. I thought I would see if he was ill, or had set the bedclothes on fire, for my mother had said that he lit his pipe under the blankets, and had warned me to run to his help if I smelt smoke in the night. I went on tiptoe through the darkness to his bedroom door, brushing against the furniture and upsetting a candlestick with a thump. When I saw there was a light in the room I felt frightened, and as I opened the door I heard grandpa shout, "Gee-up!" as loudly as a bull with a megaphone.

He was sitting straight up in bed and rocking from side to side as though the bed were on a rough road; the knotted edges of the counterpane were his reins; his invisible horses stood in a shadow beyond the bedside candle. Over a white flannel nightshirt he was wearing a red waistcoat with walnut-size brass buttons. The over-filled bowl of his pipe smoldered among his whiskers like a little burning hayrick on a stick. At the sight of me his hands dropped from the reins and lay blue and quiet, the bed stopped still on a level road, he muffled his tongue into silence, and the horses drew softly up.

"Is there anything the matter, grandpa?" I asked, though the clothes were not on fire. His face in the candlelight looked like a ragged quilt pinned upright on the black air and patched all over with goat-beards.

He stared at me mildly. Then he blew down his pipe, scattering the sparks and making a high, wet dog-whistle of the stem, and shouted: "Ask no questions."

After a pause, he said slyly: "Do you ever have nightmares, boy?"

I said: "No."

"Oh, yes, you do," he said.

I said I was woken by a voice that was shouting to horses.

"What did I tell you?" he said. "You eat too much. Who ever heard of horses in a bedroom?"

He fumbled under his pillow, brought out a small, tinkling bag, and carefully untied its strings. He put a sovereign in my hand, and said: "Buy a cake." I thanked him and wished him goodnight.

As I closed my bedroom door, I heard his voice crying loudly and gaily, "Gee-up! Gee-up!" And the rocking of the travelling bed.

Dylan Thomas: from *Portrait of the Artist as a Young Dog* (J. M. Dent, 1940), copyright © The Trustees for the copyrights of the late Dylan Thomas 1940, reproduced by permission of David Higham Associates

Passage 2

Warning
When I am an old woman I shall wear purple
With a red hat which doesn't go and doesn't suit me,
And I shall spend my pension on brandy and summer gloves
And satin sandals and say we've no money for butter.
I shall sit down on the pavement when I'm tired
And gobble up samples in shops and press alarm bells
And run my stick along the public railings
And make up for the sobriety* of my youth.
I shall go out in my slippers in the rain
And pick the flowers in other people's gardens
And learn to spit.
You can wear terrible shirts and grow more fat
And eat three pounds of sausages at a go
Or only bread and pickle for a week
And hoard pens and pencils and beermats and things in boxes.
But now we must have clothes that keep us dry
And pay our rent and not swear in the street
And set a good example for the children.
We will have friends to dinner and read the papers.
But maybe I ought to practise a little now?
So people who know me are not too shocked and surprised
When suddenly I am old and wear purple.

Jenny Joseph

Copyright – from *Selected Poems* (Bloodaxe Books, 1992), reproduced by permission of Johnson & Alcock
*sobriety = self-control

Passage 3

Budgerigars and begonias

A study reported in 1974 on the value of giving budgerigars to old people. The authors started with the premise that old people can suffer from periods of social isolation which can lead to substantial psychiatric deterioration. While they knew of some substantial work on the beneficial effect of pets on all ages, they were unaware of controlled studies, so they did one.

Budgerigars and begonias

There were five groups, but with only six old people aged between 75 and 81 years in each. Each elderly person was interviewed by a psychologist and a social worker, and asked a series of 22 questions about their life and attitude. Questions like "Do you have feelings of being fed up?" and "Do you feel time drags?" Favourable rapport was established by allowing each old person to choose a small gift, like a torch or a tray.

At this stage five interventions were set up:

1. Give a budgerigar, cage, tray and bird food to six people who had a TV set.
2. Give a begonia to six people who had a TV set.
3. Give a budgerigar, cage, tray and bird food to six people who had no TV set.
4. Give a begonia to six people who had no TV set.
5. Control group of six people, half of whom had a TV set.

The questionnaire was administered again, five months later, and items were marked as no change, favourable change or unfavourable change.

However, there were some problems:

Six of 18 old people refused a budgerigar – mainly because they didn't like seeing birds in cages. None of the old people offered a begonia refused.

Some of the budgerigars died within six weeks of placement – but most of the subjects either had another bird given them or bought one themselves.

At the time of the follow up visit only just over half of the old people could be assessed. Some had died, some had moved, and some just couldn't be contacted. So analysis was on half the original number of subjects.

Results

All 12 old people who had budgerigars had given the birds names, and insisted on making arrangements for food and so on. Some had made elaborate playgrounds and many taught the birds to speak. It was not reported whether similar attention was given to the begonias.

Having or not having a TV set made no difference, and we have combined the data from the questionnaire scores. At five months the controls had an overall unfavourable change in questionnaire scores, people given begonias had no overall change, but those given budgerigars had dramatically favourable changes in questionnaire scores.

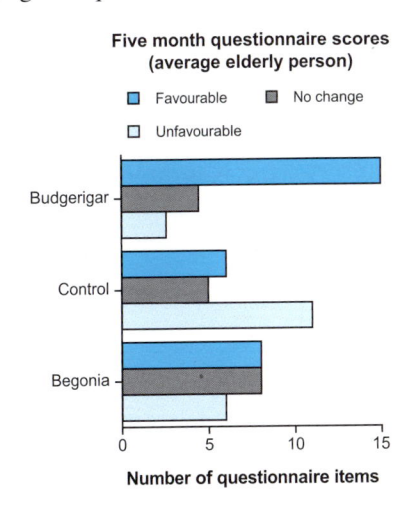

Five month questionnaire scores (average elderly person)

Comment

This trial was neither randomised, nor did it have particularly large numbers. It did show a big effect and tried hard to establish that the fact of the trial did not confound the effect of the budgerigar. The authors comment that it wasn't always so much the budgerigar itself, but the focus it made for discussion during social visits. For some of the elderly people the budgerigar stimulated visits, from local children, for instance, who came to teach the bird their names.

Reading Test

Questions 1–5 are about Passage 1, *Dylan Thomas's autobiography*.

1. Write what you learn about the character of the old man and how he explains what he is doing.
   Focus: Deduce, infer and interpret information and events or ideas from the text.

   _____
   _____
   _____
   _____
   _____
   _____
   _____
   _____
   _____
   _____

2. What does the author suggest when he describes the old man "trotting his tongue on the roof of his mouth" and "his tongue had powerful hooves"?
   Focus: Comment on the writer's use of language, grammatical and literary features (word and sentence level).

   _____
   _____
   _____
   _____
   _____
   _____
   _____

Reading Test

3 Find and quote two examples to show the noises the boy did not like in the house.

Focus: Describe, select and retrieve information and events or ideas from the text. Use quotation and reference to the text.

2

4 Comment on the effectiveness of the following: i.e. show what the descriptions add to the author's intention in the passage.

As loudly as a bull with a megaphone...

His pipe smouldered among his whiskers like a little burning hayrick on a stick...

Focus: Comment on the writer's use of language, grammatical and literary features (word and sentence level).

4

TOTAL

6

7

Reading Test

5 Show how the writer effectively creates the old man's fantasy.

You should write about:

- the changing attitude of the boy towards his grandfather
- how the boy becomes aware of what is happening and what he had been doing previously
- what the house is like
- what he hears and sees as he gets closer to the room
- what his grandfather's fantasy is and how the old man is dramatising this
- the unusual images and description used by the writer.

Focus: Identify and comment on the writer's purposes and viewpoints and the effect of the text on the reader.

Reading Test

Questions 6–10 are about Passage 2, *Warning*.

6 Find and quote a phrase from the poem that shows that the author is looking forward to a time when she is old.

Focus: Describe, select and retrieve information and events or ideas from the text. Use quotation and reference to the text.

_____

_____

_____

2

7 List four things that the poet says she will be able to do when she is old.

Focus: Describe, select and retrieve information, events or ideas from the text. Use quotation and reference to the text.

_____

_____

_____

_____

2

8 Explain how the poet contrasts what people expect of an old lady with how she would like to behave.

In your answer you should comment on:

- what the poem says in the final section about what is expected
- how the earlier images contrast with this
- how the old lady feels about this
- how the reader feels about this.

Focus: Deduce, infer and interpret information and events or ideas from the text.

_____

_____

_____

_____

_____

5

TOTAL

9

9

Reading Test

9 The poet uses the verb "gobble", *And gobble up samples in shops.*

Comment on how well you think the verb works in the characterisation of the woman.

Focus: Comment on the writer's use of language, grammatical and literary features (word and sentence level).

_____
_____
_____
_____
_____
_____
_____

10 The definition of someone who is "eccentric" is: "not following the established pattern of conduct; odd". Explain whether you think the lady in this poem deserves this description.

In your answer you should comment on:

- what you expect the established "pattern of conduct" might be for a lady such as the one in the poem
- what she would like to do and why
- how you feel about this.

Focus: Identify and comment on the writer's purposes and viewpoints and the effect of the text on the reader.

_____
_____
_____
_____
_____
_____
_____

3

6

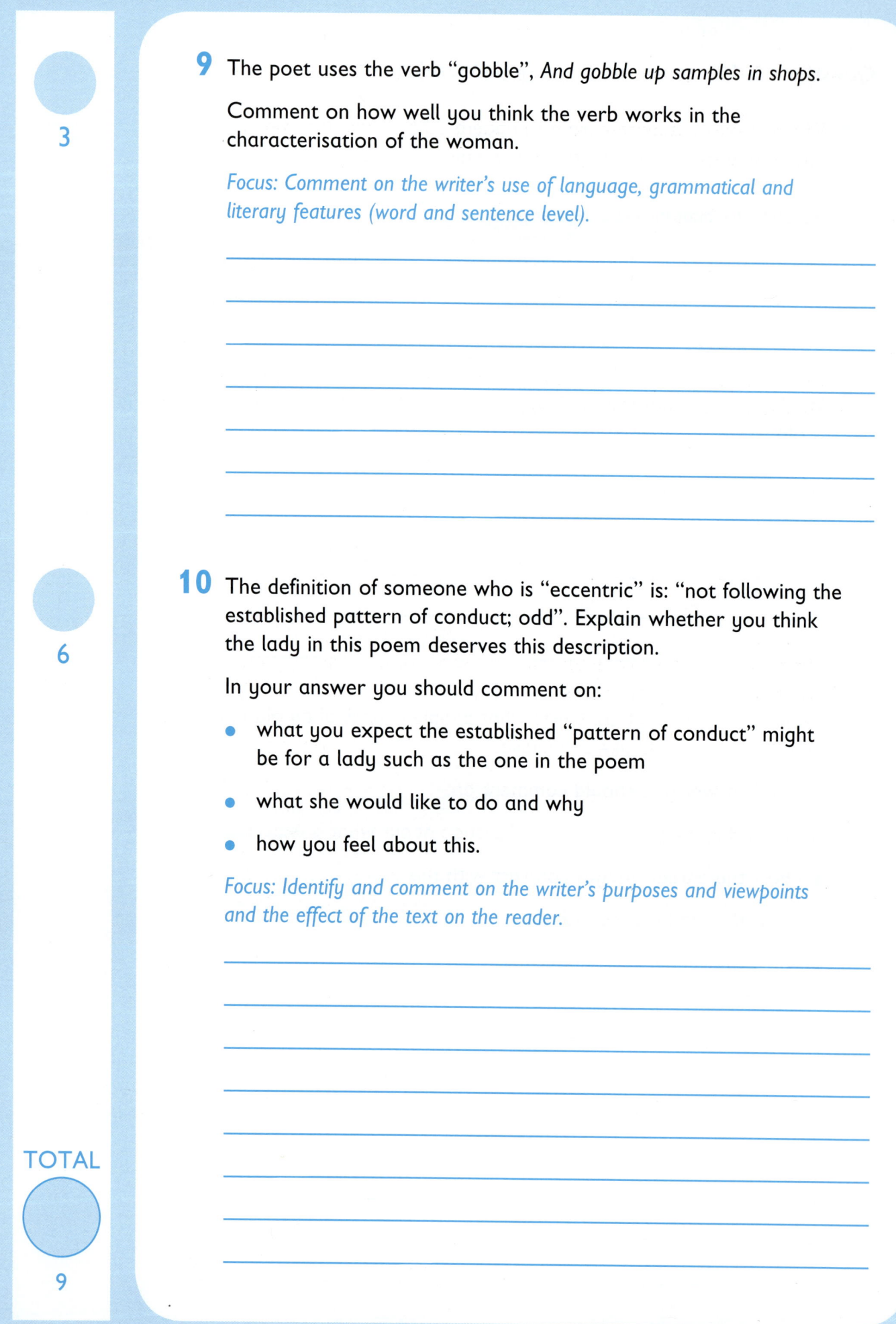

TOTAL 9

Reading Test

Questions 11–15 are about Passage 3, the *scientific journal website*.

11 What did the researchers think would be the benefit of giving old people budgerigars or begonias?
Focus: Describe, select and retrieve information and events or ideas from the text. Use quotation and reference to the text.

_____
_____

1

12 Find and quote a sentence from the passage that explains how the researchers managed to create good relationships with the old people.
Focus: Describe, select and retrieve information and events or ideas from the text. Use quotation and reference to the text.

_____
_____

1

13 What is meant by "five interventions were set up" and why do you think these were necessary?
Focus: Deduce, infer and interpret information and events or ideas from the text.

_____
_____
_____
_____

2

TOTAL

4

11

Reading Test

14 Explain what the value of the graph could be in this kind of writing and what other organisational and design features help to make the explanation clearer.

Focus: Comment on the structure and organisation of texts, grammatical and presentational features (text level).

4

15 Explain the impact on the meaning of the sentences of the words in bold in the two examples.

"The questionnaire was administered again, five months later, and items were marked as no change, favourable change or unfavourable change.

However, there were some problems."

"At five months the controls had an overall unfavourable change in questionnaire scores, people given begonias had no overall change, **but** those given budgerigars had dramatically favourable changes in questionnaire scores."

Focus: Comment on the writer's use of language, grammatical and literary features (word and sentence level).

3

TOTAL 7

Introduction to the Writing Test

This test helps you to gain an insight into your child's ability to write independently: to communicate meaning to the reader using the conventions of punctuation, spelling and handwriting.

The Level 6 internally marked English writing test consists of two tasks in a single paper:

- a Shorter Writing Task
- a Longer Writing Task.

It is recommended that children are given 20 minutes for the Shorter Writing Task and 40 minutes for the Longer Writing Task (including up to five minutes of planning time).

A planning sheet is not provided for the Shorter Writing Task, but children may use blank paper if they wish to plan. A planning sheet is provided for the Longer Task.

1. Read aloud the starting point.

2. **For fiction:** Introduce the planning sheet if available and discuss the headings on it. Emphasise the importance of:

    - writing a whole story and not just part of it
    - planning the story
    - thinking of a good opening to make the reader want to read on
    - keeping the reader interested
    - introducing the setting, the main character and the plot early in the story
    - helping the reader to get to know the characters
    - thinking of a good ending, rather than stopping abruptly.

    For information: Discuss any points on the planning sheet:

    - thinking up a good introduction to make the reader want to read on
    - keeping the reader interested
    - making the text easy for the reader to follow
    - thinking of a good ending so that the information does not just "tail off".

    You must not tell the child what to write!

3. Point out that grammar, spelling and punctuation are important.

4. Remind the child to think about punctuation and how it helps the reader to make sense of what is written.

5. If the child finishes before 60 minutes are up, encourage him or her to read through their work to look for anything that can be improved and to check grammar, spelling and punctuation.

Writing Test

The Shorter Writing Task

You should spend no longer than **20 minutes** on this.

There are **10 marks** available.

If you could change the world to improve the lives of old people what would you do? Write a speech to explain your point of view to your class.

- You should write only four paragraphs to explain your point of view and give reasons.
- Remember to use an appropriate style for a speech and aim to persuade.

You can make notes in this space.

Writing Test

The Longer Writing Task

You should spend no longer than **40 minutes** on this, including planning time.

There are **20 marks** available.

Some say that respect for the older generation is disappearing. Imagine that you work for an organisation that aims to help old people lead a fuller life in our society. Write a report about this, suggesting ways of changing the attitudes of young people.

In your answer you should:

- use the appropriate style for a report
- give your views with evidence or stories to back this up
- provide a few sensible and developed strategies for change.

Planning format:

Introduction: What is the subject of the report?	Description of the issue
Examples:	What can be done? Examples?
Language issues: Paragraphs easy to follow, include facts and opinions, mainly present tense	Conclusion:

Grammar, Punctuation and Spelling Test

The test will assess your abilities in the following technical aspects of English:

- grammar
- punctuation
- spelling
- vocabulary.

You have **40 minutes** to answer these questions.

This test is marked out of **40** but is worth **20 marks** in the final assessment.

1 Copy each sentence twice. Give each of them two different meanings by using a different preposition each time, for example: The sergeant stood **in** his sentry box. The sergeant stood **behind** his sentry box.

a) That motorway passes... the city.

_____

_____

b) A strong wind was blowing... the west.

_____

_____

c) My mum drove the jeep... the village.

_____

_____

d) Our estate agent told us to sign the contract... the line.

_____

_____

Grammar, Punctuation and Spelling Test

2 Write out the following passage correctly punctuated with apostrophes:

Lets look at the dinosaurs skeleton. Its made of hundreds of the animals bones. I cant believe theyve all come from one animals graveyard. Its makers mustve dug up loads of animals in the countrys mountains.

5

3 Here are some awkward verbs. Complete the tense chart.

Verb	Yesterday I…	I have… *No*
To swim	swam	
To write	wrote	
To begin	began	
To buy	bought	
To choose	chose	
To come	came	
To drink	drank	
To eat	ate	

8

TOTAL

13

17

Grammar, Punctuation and Spelling Test

4 Copy each sentence. Change the noun in brackets into an adjective.

a) The bush was full of (poison) berries.

b) Max made a (sense) suggestion for once.

c) It rained all week so the holiday was a (misery) experience.

d) The book was so (value) I was afraid to touch it.

e) I apologised for making such a (fool) mistake.

Grammar, Punctuation and Spelling Test

5 Write each of the following sentences again to make the meaning clear. You may need to restructure the sentence or to split each example into more than one sentence.

a) The jeweller took the chain from her neck and twisted it.

b) You will all go outside and collect the rubbish left from yesterday, including the teachers.

c) Whenever my sisters make gingerbread men for me at school, they look really happy.

d) I enjoy eating spaghetti more than my friends.

6 Explain the two meanings that each sentence could have.

6

8

TOTAL

14

Grammar, Punctuation and Spelling Test

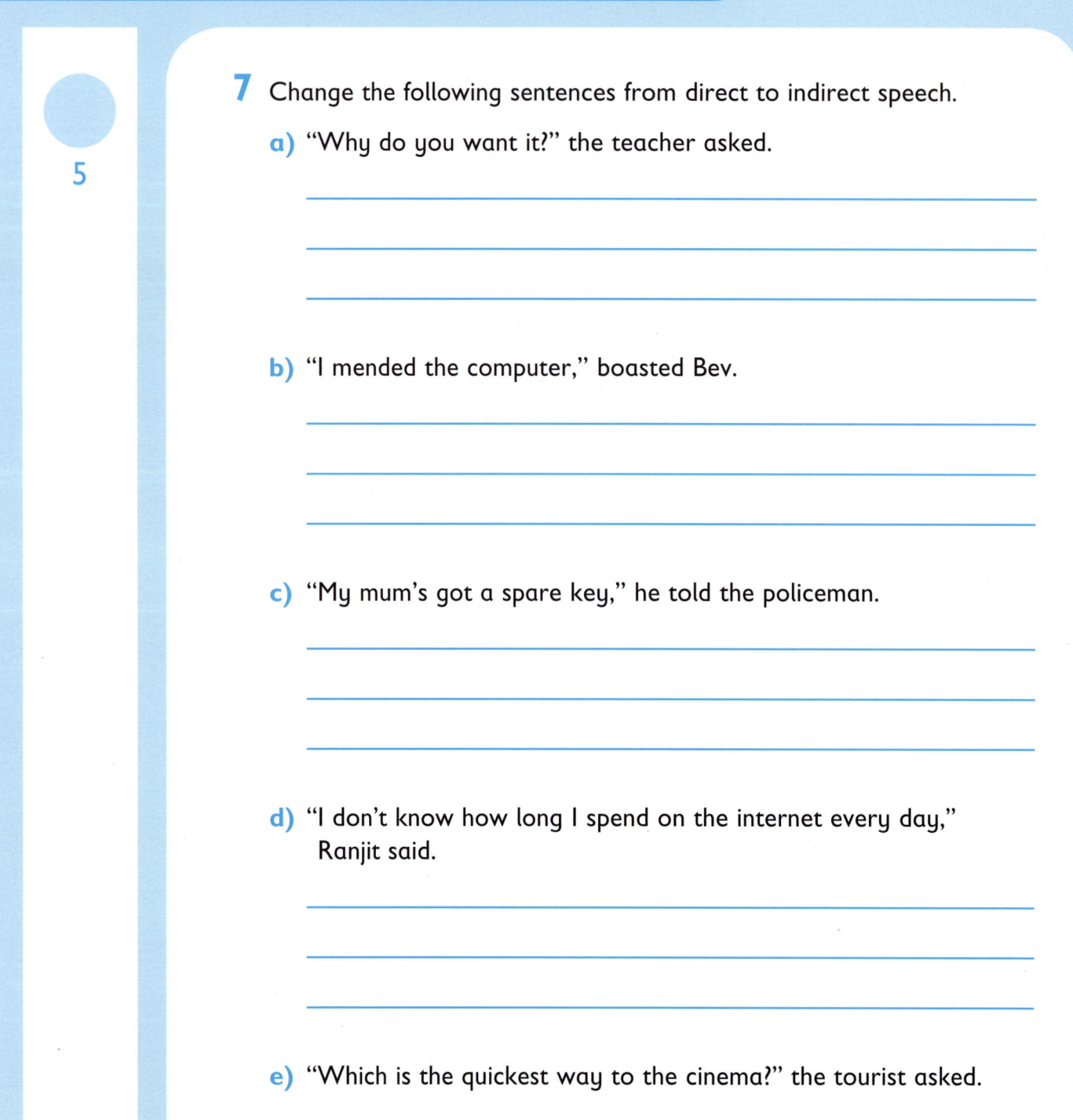

7 Change the following sentences from direct to indirect speech.

a) "Why do you want it?" the teacher asked.

b) "I mended the computer," boasted Bev.

c) "My mum's got a spare key," he told the policeman.

d) "I don't know how long I spend on the internet every day," Ranjit said.

e) "Which is the quickest way to the cinema?" the tourist asked.

Grammar, Punctuation and Spelling Test

8 Choose negative prefixes to make each of these words into antonyms.

a) justice

_____

b) polite

_____

c) approve

_____

d) behave

_____

e) literate

_____

Grammar, Punctuation and Spelling Test

9 Complete the chart.

Root verb	+ing	+ed
hop		
lag		
pin		
hope		
hug		

Grammar, Punctuation and Spelling Test

10 Copy these words and choose "ible" or "able" to complete each one.

a) poss

b) horr

c) flex

d) suit

e) agree

f) sens

g) invis

h) incred

i) understand

j) cap

Answers
Reading Test

Answers, Marking and Conversion Tables

Reading Test

It is difficult to mark answers in an English test because there is often not a "right answer" as there could be in maths. A mark scheme is provided for each question. You will need to judge how well the points made in the answer match with the score criteria. Any point should be clearly stated. Examiners should not have to dig beneath the surface to find the relevant point. The most effective way to assess work at home is to mark the piece with the candidate so both can see how the final score is calculated. This will involve discussion of what is in the answer and what has been omitted and so can form a learning experience in itself.

It is also preferable to carry out the task yourself as a parent/guardian before marking it. This will make the task clearer to you and it will also be interesting to see what score you achieve!

Questions 1–5 are about Passage 1, *Dylan Thomas's autobiography*

1 *The fantasy of the old man goes back to a scene in the wild west. He imagines he is riding a wagon down "a rough road". He is dressed for the part and is totally absorbed by this activity. This seems very eccentric for an adult, but some may feel that it is acceptable for an old person. Others may feel it is unacceptable for any adult. This gives us the impression of an old man who is perhaps senile; indeed the boy has been told to look after him because he may not be able to look after himself.*

However, the old man is in fact in control of all that he is doing. He is not shocked by the child's entry. He slowly stops and does not try to hide what he was doing. This would have caused more attention to be drawn to him. He has a firm understanding of young children – that they may be easily influenced by what an adult tells them and also by bribery.

The boy does not really comprehend what is happening at first: "Is there anything the matter, grandpa?" The image Thomas uses of the "ragged quilt" makes the old man seem even more sympathetic. However, the grandfather's strategy is very clever. He persuades the child he is having a dream. Some may feel he is a

5

TOTAL
5

Answers

devious or sly character, but his argument is a clever one. "Do you have nightmares boy?" He is in fact making a joke of it (mares are female horses) so he is enjoying the activity of getting out of the situation. Finally the old man bribes the child with money, "Buy a cake".

He is not embarrassed by being "caught"; as soon as the boy goes, he continues with his fantasy.

2 *The author awakes hearing the sound of galloping horses impersonated by his grandfather. He used these two metaphors to describe how his grandfather is making the noises. They suggest the powerful noise that he is making in his fantasy.*

3 *"The floorboards had creaked like mice… the walls had creaked like wood… curtains flapped and branches beaten against the window…"*

4 *As loudly as a bull with a megaphone… The image is vaguely ridiculous but powerful and gives a vivid impression of the loud noise. Not only is it loud but it is amplified as if the animal had a megaphone.*

His pipe smouldered among his whiskers like a little burning hayrick on a stick… The image gives us some sympathy for the old man. His pipe is overflowing with tobacco and we can see the strands burning as if hay was smoking. It also suggests the shape of the tobacco ring from the bowl of his pipe.

5 *The boy has been told that his grandfather is somewhat of a "danger" – he might set the house alight because he smokes in bed. There is also a suggestion that he "might be ill". This gives us an impression that he is old and frail. The author obviously feels that he is somewhat eccentric – he is even a little afraid of him: "I felt frightened". As a child he seems to accept the eccentric behaviour of the old man – the cowboy game he is playing is one that a young boy might play as well.*

The boy had been reading cowboy stories and had fallen asleep: "I woke from a dream full of whips… windy gallops over cactus fields… roaring and riding in a book." When he is awoken by his grandfather's noises he still thinks he is dreaming. He hears "trotting the tongue on the roof of his mouth" – making noises like a galloping horse and other "cowboy" noises. He sees a light under the door when he goes to investigate.

3

2

4

TOTAL

9

Answers

The boy is already a little afraid of the old eccentric house. The imagery is of creaking and "branches beaten against the window". He sets off in the darkness and knocks against the furniture.

When he opens the door his grandfather makes his final "gee-up" noise. He has been caught imagining that he is riding a wagon or a horse – "the counterpane… his reins". His grandfather is wearing a red waistcoat and is smoking a pipe. The old man does not stop suddenly because he has been "caught". He "muffled his tongue into silence and the horses drew softly up". He continues with the fantasy as if there is nothing wrong. He then moves through the complicated procedure of persuading the boy that he has been dreaming the whole event, but gives him some money as a bribe. As the boy leaves, the old man continues with his fantasy.

The writer makes the scene unusual by his use of imagery and description. The poet changes words into unusual verbs: "trotting his tongue on the roof of his mouth." The noises are described in two ways – the floorboards as mice; the mice as floorboards. The old man's tongue is animated: "his tongue had powerful hooves". Some of the metaphors and similes are very unusual: "his bedroom… a great meadow", "as loudly as a bull with a megaphone", "like a little burning hayrick on a stick".

7

TOTAL

7

26

Answers

Questions 6–10 are about Passage 2, *Warning*

6 "I shall wear purple…" (future tense).

"But maybe I ought to practise a little now?"

2

7 Examples include:
Wear purple… with a red hat which doesn't go
Spend her pension on brandy
Sit down on the pavement
There are many more.

2

8 The final section of the poem gives an indication of what society expects, e.g. clothes are functional – to keep her dry – not to be colourful or shocking. Her money should be spent on practical things, such as paying her rent, not on making her life pleasurable in its last stages. The way she speaks is even regulated by society's expectations, e.g. she is not expected to swear. Old people are expected to set a good example to the "younger generation" and not act in outrageous ways. However, the younger generation are permitted to do this in some way. There is a sense that this was not always the case and this old lady seems to have "missed out" on this. She will "have friends to dinner".

All the earlier images – colourful clothes, shocking activities are seen as in direct contrast to society's "normal" rules.

The lady is obviously not really old when she is writing the poem as she wants to "practise" so people will not be too shocked later. There is a sense in which she has made up her mind to do some of these things.

5

9 And gobble up samples in shops. The poet could have used a simple verb such as "eat" but this verb suggests eating greedily and without manners – all the things that she is looking forward to being able to do – to break all of society's expectations of how she should behave.

3

10 The interest in the poem lies in the fact that the narrator can fantasise about what it might be like to offend all the conventions of society. We do not know whether she will actually do any of these "shocking" things, but they appeal to our sense of the absurd. In fact there is no reason why old ladies should not behave in this way – but if they did they would be considered "eccentric".

The clothes she suggests are shocking because of their bright colours – our expectation is that old ladies should wear sober colours. She suggests spending her money on luxuries rather than

TOTAL

12

Answers

on essentials — even though our expectation is that pensioners are not very "well-off". Her actions, e.g. sitting on the pavement, playing with a stick like a child, would be out of character with our expectations of "the older generation". Generally, the old lady wants to be an individual — not bound by the rules of society. She had to make up for the "sobriety" of her youth. She will even carry out shocking things — stealing flowers, spitting, eating huge amounts of one thing.

The scene is amusing because of the contrast of our expectations, but there is also a hint of sadness in the poem. She has been restricted all he life by what society says she must do. Even in her old age she has to follow rules — in fact, there may be even more rules for older people.

Answers

Questions 11–15 are about Passage 3, the *scientific journal website*

11 They thought that these would provide a kind of "companionship" and so would stop the old people feeling isolated.

1

12 "Favourable rapport was established by allowing each old person to choose a small gift, like a torch or a tray."

1

13 "Five interventions were set up" suggests five different kinds of experiment were undertaken. These included "control" experiments, experiments to show what happens if no variables are introduced – and are necessary in science to show that the results of experiments are valid.

2

14 Graphs are visual representations of data and make complicated sets of figures easier to view and to interpret at one go. Here we have three things shown: the number of questions, the kind of responses and what was used in the experiment. Other organisational devices include: the use of subheadings, the use of bullet points and the use of numbered points. All of these make it easier for the reader to assimilate complicated information.

4

15 **However** suggests a change in perspective and the introduction of alternatives.

But suggests an alternative point of view as well.

3

TOTAL

11

Answers
Writing Test

Assessing the Writing Test

What kinds of writing will a moderator expect to see? Here is a range of types of writing. The list is not definitive and evidence is not required for every pupil in every text type.

Recount: a sequential retelling of events, e.g. a diary entry, newspaper report, factual story based on people or events.

Procedure or Instruction: stating how to do/make something, how to take care of something.

Narrative: generally a fictitious story, although may be based on fact. Can be written in different genres, e.g. adventure, science fiction, historical, ghost.

Report: describes what something is or was like and provides information about it, e.g. report on a school project, a letter, a news report.

Explanation: explains how or why something happens or works. Is usually organised logically and/or sequentially.

Argument and persuasion: presents opinion and points of view, which may be biased or balanced.

Poetry: e.g. to entertain, to reflect, to convey information, to tell a story, to share knowledge, etc.

Answers

Writing at Key Stage 2: How to judge levels

The following criteria provide guidelines to help you gain an idea of your child's writing level. Each level assumes that the criteria for the previous level have been met.

Level 3

Pupils' writing is often organised, imaginative and clear. The main features of different forms of writing are used appropriately, beginning to be adapted to different readers. Sequences of sentences extend ideas logically and words are chosen for variety and interest. The basic grammatical structure of sentences is usually correct. Spelling is usually accurate, including that of common, polysyllabic words. Punctuation to mark sentences – full stops, capital letters and question marks – is used accurately. Handwriting is joined and legible.

Level 4

Pupils' writing in a range of forms is lively and thoughtful. Ideas are often sustained and developed in interesting ways and organised appropriately for the purpose of the reader. Vocabulary choices are often adventurous and words are used for effect. Pupils are beginning to use grammatically complex sentences, extending meaning. Spelling, including that of polysyllabic words that conform to regular patterns, is generally accurate. Full stops, capital letters and question marks are used correctly, and pupils are beginning to use punctuation within the sentence. Handwriting style is fluent, joined and legible.

Level 5

Pupils' writing is varied and interesting, conveying meaning clearly in a range of forms for different readers, using a more formal style where appropriate. Vocabulary choices are imaginative and words are used precisely. Simple and complex sentences are organised into paragraphs. Words with complex regular patterns are usually spelt correctly. A range of punctuation, including commas, apostrophes and inverted commas, is usually used accurately. Handwriting is joined, clear and fluent and, where appropriate, is adapted to a range of tasks.

Level 6

Pupils' writing often engages and sustains the reader's interest, showing some adaptation of style and register to different forms, including using an impersonal style where appropriate. Pupils use a range of sentence structures and varied vocabulary to create effects. Spelling is generally accurate, including that of irregular words. Handwriting is neat and legible. A range of punctuation is usually used correctly to clarify meaning, and ideas are organised into paragraphs.

Answers

For purposes of comparison at this higher level, we have included Level 5 and Level 6 criteria for assessing writing.

What does a Level 5 look like in writing?

The following simplified descriptions will help you to gain an idea of your child's level in writing. They are provided for teachers by the Standards and Testing Agency.

Composition and effect	Text structure and organisation	Sentence structure and punctuation
• Purpose of writing is clear and generally maintained with some effective selection and placing of content to inform/engage the reader. • Features of selected form are clearly established (appropriate selection and variation of tense, choice of person, level of formality, adaptation of content for genre and audience…). • Content is balanced and controlled, e.g. some effective selection and placing of content to engage the reader (placement of significant idea/event for emphasis, reflective comment, opinion, dialogue…). • Established and controlled viewpoint with some development of opinion, attitude, position or stance. • Ideas developed through elaboration, nominalisation, imaginative detail, precise vocabulary. Varied stylistic features may support both purpose and effect (alliteration, metaphors, puns, emotive words, vivid language).	• Overall organisation of text is supported by paragraphs or sections which enable coherent development and control of content across the text. • Relationships between paragraphs or sections give structure to the whole text e.g. links make structure between topics clear; connections between opening and ending. • Sequencing and structured organisation of paragraphs and/or sections contributes to overall effectiveness of text. • Information/events developed in greater depth within paragraphs and/or sections. • Some shaping of paragraphs may be evident to highlight or prioritise information, provide chronological links, build tension or interject comment or reflection. • A range of cohesive devices used to develop or elaborate ideas both within and between paragraphs e.g. pronouns, adverbials, connectives, subject specific vocabulary, phrases or chains of reference (*However, it should be stated… Biological changes… Despite their heroic efforts…*).	• Variety in sentence length, structure and subject to help expand ideas, convey key issues/facts or provide emphasis, detail and description. • Different sentence types, e.g. questions, direct/reported speech, commands (*turn upside down*) used appropriately. • A range of subordinate connectives (*whilst, until, despite*) with possible use of several subordinate clauses to aid economy of expression (*Because of their courageous efforts, all of the passengers were saved, which was nothing short of a miracle… "Whilst under my roof, you will obey my rules, which are clearly displayed"*). • Emphasis may be created through word order, accurate adaptation of verb phrases, and use of passive (*the centre has been visited often*). • A range of verb forms develops meaning and maintains appropriate tense choice (*it will probably leave of its own accord… we could catch a later train, but will we arrive on time?*). • Additional words and phrases contribute to shades of meaning, e.g. adverbs (*extremely*). • Range of punctuation used, almost always correctly, e.g. brackets, dashes, colons.

Answers

What does a Level 6 look like in writing?

The following simplified descriptions will help you to gain an idea of your child's level in writing. They are provided for teachers by the Standards and Testing Agency.

Composition and effect	Text structure and organisation	Sentence structure and punctuation
• Able to write with confidence and imagination. Can adapt writing to different forms, purposes and audience (a persuasive speech which shocks the listener, a narrative that focuses on the perpetrator's perspective, a magazine column that is used to comment on moral/social issues). Varying levels of formality are adopted according to purpose and audience (appropriate use of controlled informality, shifts between formal narrative and informal dialogue). • Viewpoint is convincing and generally sustained throughout a piece (e.g. authoritative expert view, convincing characterisation, opposing opinions). • Ideas are developed through controlled use of elaboration, nominalisation and imaginative detail. Vocabulary is varied and often ambitious. A range of stylistic features contribute to the effect of the text (e.g. rhetorical questions, repetition, figurative language).	• Overall organisation of the text is controlled to take account of the reader's possible reaction/questions/opinion (e.g. use of flashback in narrative, placing of information according to importance, balancing perspectives or points of view, sequencing of events or ideas). • A range of features are used to inform the reader of the overall direction of the writing (e.g. opening paragraphs clearly introduce themes or create interest, withholding of information for effect, paragraph or sentence markers, references link information/ideas across the text). • Some paragraphs and/or sections are shaped and developed to support meaning and purpose (priority subjects/events/ideas developed in greater detail and depth). • A range of cohesive devices contribute to the effect of the text on the reader and the placing of emphasis for impact (e.g. precise adverbials as sentence starters, a range of appropriate connectives, subject specific vocabulary, select use of pronoun referencing, complex noun phrases, prepositional phrases).	• Controlled use of a variety of simple and more complex sentences contribute to clarity of purpose and overall effect on the reader. • A range of sentence features are used to give clarity or emphasis of meaning (fronted adverbials: *As a consequence of... Glancing backwards... Some weeks later...*/complex noun phrases: *The mysterious young girl in the portrait...*/prepositional phrases: *From behind the bike shed... In the event of...*). • Subordinate connectives may be manipulated for emphasis or to nominalise for succinctness (*Because of that, he failed...*). • Verb forms are mostly controlled and are consistently adapted to the form of writing (*It would be helpful if you could let me know, as this will enable me to take further action...*). • Additional words and phrases are used for precision and impact (*exceptional result, insignificant amount*) • Syntax and full range of punctuation are consistently accurate in a variety of sentence structures, with occasional errors in ambitious structures.

33

Answers

Grammar, Punctuation and Spelling Test

Answers	Marks
1. a) That motorway passes… the city. (under, over, by, through) b) A strong wind was blowing… the west. (in, through, from) c) My mum drove the jeep… the village. (through, by, in) d) Our estate agent told us to sign the contract… the line. (on, by, under)	1 mark for each different meaning/out of 8 Some leeway allowed on these responses.
2. Let's look at the dinosaur's skeleton. It's made of hundreds of the animal's bones. I can't believe they've all come from one animals' graveyard. Its makers must've dug up loads of animals in the country's mountains.	Half a mark for each correct apostrophe and half for not putting an apostrophe in "its makers"/out of 5
3. swim – swam – swum; write – wrote – written; begin – began – begun; buy – bought – bought; choose – chose – chosen; come – came – come; drink – drank – drunk; eat – ate – eaten	Half a mark each/out of 8
4. poison – poisonous; sense – sensible; misery – miserable; value – valuable; fool – foolish	1 mark each/out of 5
5. a) The jeweller twisted the chain after taking it from her neck. b) Everybody, including the teachers, will go outside and collect the rubbish left from yesterday. c) My sisters always look really happy whenever they make gingerbread men for me at school. d) Compared to my friends, I enjoy eating spaghetti more. [Or I enjoy eating spaghetti more than my friends do.]	One and a half marks each to change the sentences/out of 6 There may be some leeway on these answers as the explanations are often difficult. Give marks for clarity.

Answers

Answers	Marks
6. a) Did he twist the neck of the girl or did he twist the chain? b) Everybody including the teachers will go outside to collect the refuse – or the teachers are classed as rubbish themselves? c) Are the sisters looking happy or do their gingerbread men have smiles on their faces? d) Compared to his friends he enjoys eating spaghetti more? Or has he been eating his friends and they taste better than spaghetti?	2 marks each/out of 8 There may be some leeway on these answers as the explanations are often difficult. Give marks for clarity.
7. a) The teacher asked why he or she wanted it. b) Bev boasted that she had mended the computer. c) He told the policeman that his mum had a spare key. d) Ranjit said that he didn't know how long he spent on the internet every day. e) The tourist asked which was the quickest way to the cinema.	1 mark each/out of 5 Look for removal of speech marks and changes of tense and pronouns.
8. injustice; impolite; disapprove; misbehave; illiterate	1 mark each/out of 5
9. hop, hopping, hopped; lag, lagging, lagged; pin, pinning, pinned; hope, hoping, hoped; hug, hugging, hugged	Half a mark each/out of 5
10. possible; horrible; flexible; suitable; agreeable; sensible; invisible; incredible; understandable; capable	Half a mark each/out of 5
TOTAL: Divide by 3 so score is out of 20	

35

National Curriculum Levels – Level 6

Assessment of children's attainment in National Curriculum tests depends upon the judgement of professionals. For the purpose of this book, a simplified system of marking is used. Guidelines to National Curriculum levels provided should be regarded as a rough guide only.

Use the conversion tables below to gain an idea of whether your child has achieved a Level 6 or not.

English – reading		English – writing		English – grammar, punctuation and spelling		English – overall	
1–20	Level 6 not achieved	1–14	Level 6 not achieved	1–9	Level 6 not achieved	1–44	Level 6 not achieved
21–50	Level 6 achieved	15–30	Level 6 achieved	10–20	Level 6 achieved	45–100	Level 6 achieved

Enter your child's results below:

English – reading	English – writing	English – grammar, punctuation and spelling	English – overall
Mark	Mark	Mark	Mark

Level 6 achieved or not?

Remember, gaining a Level 6 is quite an achievement as it means that the child is working at the level of an average 14-year-old.

Notes

Notes